STEVE PARISH

MELBOURNE
Victoria · Australia

STEVE PARISH PUBLISHING PTY LTD

STEVE PARISH

MELBOURNE

Victoria · Australia

STEVE PARISH PUBLISHING PTY LTD

Introduction

V isitors to Melbourne are rarely disappointed. Set astride the quiet waters of the Yarra River and at the apex of Port Phillip Bay, the city is a successful blend of the old and new. Gleaming tall glass and steel structures mix with the remnants of fine nineteenth-century bluestone buildings. Wide, well-planned roadways radiate from the city centre with its European-inspired, tree-lined boulevards. The neat, distinctive suburbs are home to over three million people. With ample parks and gardens to provide respite from the busy streets, this urban conglomerate is a metropolis of world standard. It is little wonder that Melbourne was recently proclaimed the 'world's most livable city'.

But Melbourne has many dimensions: the city is the industrial capital of Australia, home to top corporations, and an influential centre for the arts and sport. It was also the city I was brought up in and I can well remember gazing out towards Port Phillip Bay and dreaming about the wonders of the sea.

The arts flourish in Melbourne. Apart from the more traditional ballet, opera and music, there is a vibrant sub-culture which is evident from just a brief stroll through the streets. The profusion of public art, including sculpture, decorated trams and street performers attests to this. There is also a thriving visual arts scene, from the acclaimed National Gallery of Victoria to the tiniest private display space and even the 'pavement art', likely to be encountered in the city. In fact, the National Gallery holds the largest collection of art in the Southern Hemisphere and houses many of the grand masters as well as indigenous and contemporary art.

On the weekends in winter, scarfed football fans, decked out in team colours, flock to local sports grounds to barrack for their favourite sides in that Melbourne institution, Aussie Rules. While cricket has long been the mainstay for summer sport the city also prides itself on the variety of world-class sporting events held. For over 100 years it has been the venue for Australia's richest horse race, the Melbourne Cup; it hosts the Australian Open Tennis Championship; and, more recently, it has secured the Australian Grand Prix Formula One championship.

At a more sedate pace, trams ply the streets carrying commuters on weekdays and delivering weekend shoppers to the city and those distinctive suburbs that trade on their ethnic and cultural identities. From atop the city's tallest building, the Rialto Towers, it is possible can get a feel for the size and shape of Melbourne. The sprawl of red-roofed houses and cityscapes contrasts visually with views over Port Phillip Bay, providing a balance of urban landscape and natural beauty that may surprise visitors.

Melbourne is a shopper's paradise. Large department stores compete with specialty shops, while arcades intertwine with retail centres to cater for the most material of cravings. To make the most of Melbourne, visitors should take time to explore the suburban precincts which give the city its unique flavour. In the village-like suburbs are found the best food, drinks, clothes, in fact, anything they are likely to desire. The cultural diversity of the many recent arrivals has infused the local culture with an exciting European and Asian dynamic. Southgate, the arts and leisure district across the river from the city, is Melbourne's 'Left Bank'.

Variety is the basis of the city's cafe and restaurant life and at night, in the most vibrant suburbs, Melbourne comes alive. The city skyline sparkles with office lights as the orange, evening sky gives way to the dark of night. Theatres present a variety of shows, while nightspots resonate to the latest music and the streets around the entertainment centres throng with pedestrians.

The city is surrounded by a diversity of natural attractions frequented by locals and visitors alike. Stretching south towards the horizon in two directions are peninsulas which practically join again to form an inland sea which is surrounded by over 200 kilometres of beaches. Phillip Island is home to the seasonal Penguin Parade, while the brightly-painted bathing boxes at Brighton on Port Phillip Bay give a unique look to this seaside suburb. East of Melbourne, the Yarra Valley vineyards are a popular day trip, as are the Dandenong Ranges for those wishing to get away from the city to explore the forests of giant mountain ash and delight in the cool ferny glades. Further afield, running past the spectacular Otway Ranges to the southwest, is the Great Ocean Road, one of the world's great scenic drives. Here large rock formations stand in crashing waves adjacent to the huge cliffs which skirt the sea.

In discarding its tag as 'The Garden State' and adopting the new slogan 'Victoria, On The Move', officials have tried to express the positivism which permeates the state as the turn of a new century draws near. Perhaps it is because Melbourne has largely retained its nineteenth-century charm, while at the same time adapting to the realities of late twentieth-century life, that it is able to go forward with such optimism. Or maybe it is the cosmopolitan mix of people who inhabit the place which ensures a vitality in all aspects of life. In any case, most people just enjoy this handsome, energetic and cultivated city.

Steve Parish

Pages 2-3: Flinders Street Station, dating from 1910, is a hub
for the railway network and a popular meeting place.
Pages 4-5: The city lights up as evening descends to nightfall.
Page 6: Stilt-walkers in the Moomba Parade, one of Melbourne's many annual festivals.
Pages 8-9: An aerial view of the city looking towards Port Phillip Bay.
Page 12: A sample of Melbourne's diverse architecture.

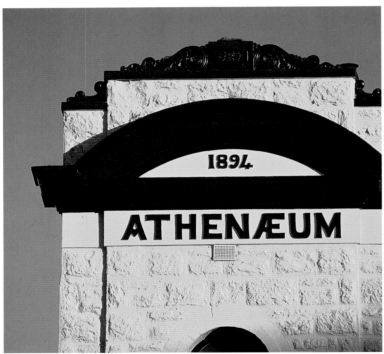

1894

ATHENÆUM

MELBOURNE EXHIBITION CENTRE

Contents

Introduction	10	Sport	95
The Yarra River	21	Eating Out	100
The Princes Bridge	26	Melbourne's Suburbs	106
Polly Woodside	29	St Kilda	111
Southgate	30	Brighton	117
Westgate Bridge	37	The Dandenongs	120
The City	38	Healesville Sanctuary	125
Shopping Around	50	Frankston	126
The Queen Victoria Market	61	Mornington Peninsula	129
Melbourne Central	62	Sorrento	135
Trams	64	Point Nepean	137
The Streets of Melbourne	67	Phillip Island	138
St Pauls Cathedral	70	Williamstown	143
Flinders Street Station	72	Bellarine Peninsula	145
The Princess' Theatre	74	The Otway Ranges	147
Victorian Arts Centre	77	The Twelve Apostles	148
Old Melbourne Gaol	78	Sovereign Hill	150
Historic Melbourne	81	Bright	153
Shrine of Remembrance	83	Winter in the Mountains	154
Royal Botanic Gardens	84	Country Victoria	157
Royal Melbourne Zoo	93	The Murray River	158

Swanston Street, looking towards St Kilda Road and the Shrine of Remembrance.

Swanston Street, with a fine example of Melbourne's public art.

The Yarra River

In 1837, an overland traveller wrote of Melbourne that "The site of the town is very pretty and well chosen...on the Yarra Yarra River...". Since then, the Yarra has continued to be the heart of Melbourne, its meandering course 'straightened' in 1897, and its green banks alternately built-upon and beautified over the years. Today, the river flows quietly through the city, past the impressive Southgate complex, its shining surface reflecting its elegant surroundings.

Top: The Yarra hosts many rowing events. *Bottom:* Relaxing on the river bank.
Opposite: City buildings framed by the arch of Southgate footbridge.
Pages 16-17: The Yarra River reflecting the city skyline at dawn.
Pages 18-19: A coxless four practise on the tranquil Yarra River.

The Princes Bridge

Spanning the Yarra River between the central business district and leafy St Kilda Road, the Princes Bridge is an elegant structure of high Victorian design. Visitors have long paused on this bridge to admire scenery up and down the river. As well as a busy route for city traffic, it is a major route for pedestrians accessing the Southbank complex and the adjacent Arts Centre.

Above: Trams crossing the Princes Bridge. *Opposite:* A Venetian-style gondola on the Yarra River.
Pages 22-23: Rowers in the morning fog, Yarra River.
Pages 24-25: Strolling the banks of the Yarra River while the morning fog lifts.

Polly Woodside

On the riverfront near Spencer Street Bridge, the Polly Woodside Maritime Park and Museum is a popular attraction for locals and visitors alike. The three-masted barque was built in Belfast in 1885. After years as a coal-carrying vessel between Europe and South America she ended her working days as a hulk. Now restored as a museum centre-piece, 'Polly' stands as a reminder of the adventure and trials of a rich maritime past.

Above: From stern to bow, Polly Woodside is shipshape again.
Opposite: The iron-hulled Polly Woodside, now one of Melbourne's most popular attractions.

Southgate

On the opposite side of the river to the central business district, the former railway goods' yard is now home to the impressive Southgate complex. It sits adjacent to the Arts complex and is only a short stroll from the National Gallery of Victoria. An arched footbridge across the Yarra joins the complex to the city. Three levels of speciality shops, restaurants and cafes provide a variety of shopping and dining experiences, while the riverside walk is a popular place to promenade on the weekend. Public artworks line the river bank and on Sunday there is an art and craft market. The new Sheraton Towers Hotel and adjoining office buildings are recent additions.

Above: The footbridge from Southgate to Flinders Walk.
Opposite: Southgate and the Yarra River viewed from Princes Bridge.
Pages 32-33: Visitors making the most of a fine weekend at the Southgate complex.

Top: Southbank Promenade. *Bottom:* Roulette is popular at the nearby Crown Casino.
Opposite: Sculpture on Southbank Promenade, with the city in the background.

Westgate Bridge

The Westgate Bridge spans the Yarra River and joins the city with the south-western suburbs and Geelong. The views from the bridge encompass the city, suburbs and Port Phillip Bay. The industrial and maritime heartland of the city, Port Melbourne has resisted the gentrification of other inner-city suburbs and retained its practical nature. However, Bay Street has been recognised for its heritage value and many of the buildings are undergoing restoration.

Top: Melbourne Docks, gateway to the State's trade.
Bottom: Westgate Bridge spanning the Yarra River.
Opposite: Westgate Bridge at dusk reflected
in the stillness of the Yarra.

The City

Melbourne can lay claim to a style and charm unique in Australia. Fine old buildings sit in well-planned surrounds while modern skyscrapers jostle for attention on the skyline. When the sun is at the right angle, the tall glass-fronted buildings often reflect their surroundings. At night, the city lights up and presents a multi-coloured display that forms a backdrop to the activities of those seeking entertainment or a good night on the town.

Above: Framed by palms, the city skyline at dusk is guarded by the statue of the Marquis of Linlithgow.
Opposite: Central city office towers basking in the morning light.
Pages 40-41: The city and suburbs from the Rialto Observation Deck.

Above: An aerial view of the city looking north over Royal Botanic Gardens and Government House.

Above: A view of the city looking northeast over Westgate Freeway.

Above: The evening city skyline and Princess' Theatre from Parliament Gardens.
Opposite: Building reflections from an aerial perspective.

Melbourne manages to successfully blend the old with the new. Office towers mix with the remnants of fine nineteenth-century bluestone buildings to create an ambience which is unique in Australia. Ample public parks and gardens are the lungs of the city and places of quietude frequented by both city workers and visitors. Radiating out from the city centre stretch the suburbs, many of them distinctive urban enclaves which are sought out as shopping and dining places.

Above: An aerial view of the city looking towards Port Phillip Bay.
Opposite: Looking south over Carlton Gardens, the Exhibition Buildings and the city towards Port Phillip Bay.
Pages 48-49: Nightfall over Melbourne.

Shopping Around

Melbourne is the retail capital of Australia and a veritable shopper's paradise. In the city you will find department stores, a huge variety of shops and retail complexes, all interwoven with a labyrinth of arcades and lanes. The village-like suburbs allow for distinctive shopping experiences of their own. The outer regions have huge shopping malls, while the inner suburbs often specialise, for instance: Bridge Road and Swan Street in Richmond for clothes; Chapel Street, South Yarra, for exclusive boutiques; Brunswick Street, Fitzroy, for bric-a-brac; and High Street, Armadale, for antiques.

Above left: Collins Place, Melbourne City. *Above right:* 234 Collins Street, Melbourne City.
Opposite: The Jam Factory, Chapel Street, South Yarra. *Pages 54-55:* High Street, Armadale.

Top: The former Commercial Bank of Australia. *Bottom:* The Block Arcade.

Above: The Royal Arcade.

Top: Jianni Studio, Chapel Street, South Yarra.
Bottom: Granny's Market, High Street, Armadale.

Top: Andrew Farmer Antiques, High Street, Armadale.
Bottom: Granny Green's Sassafras Shop, Dandenong Ranges.

Top: Morgans, Chapel Street, South Yarra.
Bottom: Armadale Flowers, High Street, Armadale.

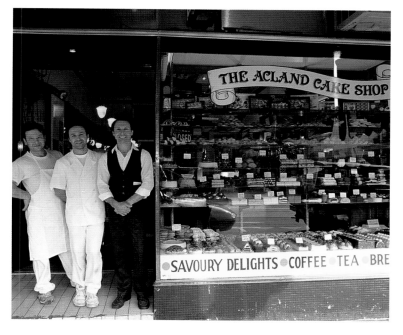

Top left: The Acland Cake Shop, Acland Street, St Kilda.
Top right: Nelson Renaissance, Nelson Place, Williamstown.
Bottom left: A fruit stall in the city.
Bottom right: Rockey's, Chapel Street, South Yarra.

Top: Fruit and vegetable seller, Queen Victoria Market.
Bottom: Seafood stall, Queen Victoria Market.

The Queen Victoria Market

Visitors come to stand in awe at this bustling, chaotic retail centre but locals come to shop, shop, shop. The market has been trading on this site for over 100 years. As the city's largest market, over 1000 traders offer everything from fresh produce, including seafood, poultry, fruit and vegetables, to plants, carpets—you name it, it's here.

Top: Delicatessen, Queen Victoria Market.
Bottom: Just of one of the crowded aisles in
what locals affectionately call the 'Vicky Markets'.

Melbourne Central

Nowhere in Melbourne does the old and new come together so dramatically as at Melbourne Central. The Latrobe Street shopping and office complex houses speciality shops and Daimaru, the Japanese department store. The feature of the centre is a 65-metre conical glass tower, built around an old shot tower which dates from the last century. The shops are located in semi-circular atrium levels around the shot tower, which serves as a very fine eating and meeting place, and a novelty clock which entertains shoppers.

Top: Looking up at the glass dome with the top of the shot tower and a hot air balloon.
Bottom: The exterior of Melbourne Central. *Opposite:* The interior of Melbourne Central.

Trams

Horse-drawn trams gave way to cable trams in 1885 before being superseded by electric models in the 1920s. One of the few cities in the world with the foresight to retain trams as a means of public transport, Melbourne has gone further and used them as vehicles for public art. Artists have been invited to treat the tram as a 'canvas' and the results are nothing short of amazing. The familiar rattle of the older trams has been largely replaced by the hum of the clean, new models which transport commuters and sight-seers on their journeys efficiently and quietly.

Top: Art is literally everywhere in Melbourne.
Bottom: Both new and old trams ply the streets.
Opposite: Looking south down St Kilda Road to the Shrine of Remembrance.

The Streets of Melbourne

Strolling the streets of Melbourne city, taking in the multitude of sights, can be exhausting. Fortunately, the wide boulevards, with large blocks, and narrow lanes have lots to see. Many visitors make use of the burgundy-coloured free trams which run around the city in a loop. A glance at the faces in the street will reveal the diversity of nationalities of the people who call Melbourne home.

Above: A pavement artist puts the finishing touches to a masterwork of public art.
Opposite: Top left: St Michaels Church and Hyatt Hotel; *Top right:* Corner of Elizabeth Street and Latrobe Street.
Centre, left and right: Bourke Street Mall. *Bottom left:* Collins Street; *Bottom right:* Swanston Street.
Pages 68-69: The 'Paris End' of Collins Street at night.

St Pauls Cathedral

St Pauls Cathedral, in Swanston Walk, is a Melbourne landmark. It stands on the site of the city's first church service. Designed by English architect William Butterworth, this classic of Gothic Revival architecture was built between 1877 and 1891, a time of great prosperity in Victoria. The towers were added in 1931. The interior is particularly impressive with intricate tiled floors, carved woodwork, detailed stonework and magnificent stained-glass windows.

Above: St Pauls Cathedral, Swanston Walk, with the city towers in the background.
Opposite: The interior of St Pauls.

Flinders Street Station

Completed in 1910, Flinders Street Station was built on the site of an earlier terminus and designed in High Victorian style. The hub of local rail services, the station has long been a meeting place due to its central location on the corner of Swanston Street and Flinders Street, at the southern boundary of Melbourne's central business district.

Above: The main entrance to Flinders Street Station on the corner of Swanston Street and Flinders Street.

The Princess' Theatre

One of the world's grand old theatres, the Princess' Theatre in
Spring Street has been restored to its former glory. The
flamboyant architecture was designed so that the building
would appear as a 'palace' for the arts, at a time when live
theatre was one of the greatest attractions. As the venue for
many of the major musical productions, the Princess enjoys
packed houses for most of these performances.

Above: A glittering palace, the princess of live theatre.

Victorian Arts Centre

Just a short walk along St Kilda Road from the city centre, over Princes Bridge, is the cultural centre of Melbourne. The National Gallery of Victoria, opened in 1968, is surrounded by a 15-metre wide moat and holds the largest collection of art in the Southern Hemisphere. Nearby, the Victorian Arts Centre, completed in 1984, is the centre of a cultural precinct which draws performers from all over the world. Beneath the arts centre spire is the State Theatre, the Playhouse and the George Fairfax Studio. Closer to the Yarra River is the Melbourne Concert Hall.

Above: 'Angel', a sculpture by Deborah Halpern outside the National Gallery of Victoria.
Opposite: The distinctive spire of the Theatre Building of the Victorian Arts Centre, framed by the trees alongside St Kilda Road.

Old Melbourne Gaol

The old bluestone gaol, built in 1841, is now a penal museum. This foreboding place is a gruesome reminder of the realities of penal life; the prison was the scene of 104 hangings before it was closed in 1923. The centrepiece of the complex is the gallows, although it is worth remembering that many prisoners served their time without incident and others, often transportees from England, were to serve extra time here for petty offences.

Top: Ned Kelly's suit of armour, one of four sets in existence.
Bottom: A reconstruction of the 1880 hanging of Ned Kelly, Melbourne Gaol's most notorious prisoner.
Opposite: The Cell Block at Old Melbourne Gaol.

Historic Melbourne

Melbournites have long been aware of the importance of their heritage buildings. Established and consolidated during the reign of Queen Victoria (1837-1901), the city is one of the finest examples of a Victorian city remaining anywhere in the world. The wealth generated from gold and wool was the basis for a series of building booms, which saw some magnificent private, commercial and public buildings. These stand today as a testament to grand nineteenth-century architecture. Como House is an example of the town residences built by the 'squattocracy' in the second half of the century, while Parliament House remains as a superb example of the public buildings which were constructed during the period.

Top: Como House, a colonial mansion dating from 1847,
set in fine grounds at South Yarra.
Bottom: The historic Hotel Windsor, Melbourne's
grandest old hotel.
Opposite: The fine old Parliament House, built in
1856, in the evening light.

Shrine of Remembrance

This grand war memorial was originally constructed as a shrine to Victoria's war dead from World War I. The forecourt was built in 1952, in memory of the fallen from World War II. It has been designed so that a shaft of light, entering through an opening in the ceiling, strikes the Rock of Remembrance in the inner sanctuary, on Remembrance Day each year. Today, it stands as a memorial to the dead of all wars. The Shrine is the centre-piece of Anzac Day commemorations on 25 April each year.

Above: The Shrine of Remembrance and Perpetual Flame at night.
Opposite: A view over the Shrine of Remembrance, looking down St Kilda Road to Swanston Street and central-city Melbourne.

Royal Botanic Gardens

Melbourne's early administrators established the tradition of beautifying the city's streets and reserved large areas of land for public parks and gardens. Not far from the heart of the city, the Royal Botanic Gardens, covering over 35 hectares, forms a part of Melbourne's extensive public garden domain. Created in the English landscaping tradition of the eighteenth century, the rolling lawns, wooded coppices and formal flower gardens are a delight to locals and visitors alike. Other gardens are: Kings Domain, which contains Government House and the Shrine of Remembrance; Carlton Gardens, which surround the Exhibition Buildings; and Fitzroy Gardens, the site of Captain Cook's Cottage, a Conservatory and a model Tudor village.

Above: A family of swans gather for the offerings of visitors to the Gardens.
Opposite: Feeding the ducks, Royal Botanic Gardens.
Pages 86-87: An aerial view over Government House and the Royal Botanic Gardens looking south-east.

Above: Marquis of Linlithgow statue, Kings Domain.
Annual displays of floral garden art are a feature of the
public parks and gardens around Melbourne.

Above: Captain Cook's Cottage, Fitzroy Gardens. The home of Cook's parents, this building
was dismantled and moved from Yorkshire to its present site in 1934.
It is furnished in the manner of a mid-eighteenth-century English cottage.

Above: Conservatory and 'Diana and the Hounds' statue, Fitzroy Gardens.
The elegant art-deco exterior of this building is in pleasing contrast
to the riotous floral display of its interior.

90

Above: Inside the Conservatory, Fitzroy Gardens.
The floral display in this fine building, which was completed in 1928,
is typical of the effort gardens' staff put into their work.

Royal Melbourne Zoological Gardens

Melbourne Zoo, the oldest zoo in Australia, was opened in 1862 and is today one of the city's top attractions. Planned so that animals are in surroundings that resemble their natural habitat as closely as possible, Melbourne Zoo is home to more than 350 Australian and exotic animals. A notable success has been the breeding in captivity of some of the world's endangered species including the Lowland Gorilla.

Top left: A Sumatran tiger. *Top right:* An African lion.
Bottom left: The Butterfly House. *Bottom right:* A Lowland Gorilla.
Opposite: A tranquil corner, Japanese Gardens, Melbourne Zoo.

Sport

Melbournians are passionate about all sports and particularly their code of football. Each week of the season, decked out in their club's colours, they crowd the stands to barrack for their favourite teams. The Melbourne Cricket Ground becomes the mecca for cricket in Victoria in summer. Melbourne is also host to the Australian leg of the world Formula One motor racing championship; the nation's most famous horse race, the Melbourne Cup; and the Australian Open tennis competition.

Above: Crowds flock to the Melbourne Cricket Ground for the AFL Grand Final.
Opposite: Fans crowd the stands at the Melbourne Cricket Ground to barrack for their favourite team.
Page 96-97: The big men fly in a clash for the ball in this Australian Rules Football match between Carlton and Geelong.

Above: Formula One racing cars performing on the Albert Park circuit during the Australian Grand Prix.
Opposite Top: Cricket is the big event for sports lovers in summer.
Opposite Bottom: Jockeys and horses turn into the straight for the final sprint to the
finish of Australia's richest horse race, the Melbourne Cup.

Eating Out

People in Melbourne have made an art form out of dining out. Wherever diners go, they are astounded by the range and quality of food available and find food from the cultures of people from all over the world. For instance: Lonsdale Street in the city for Greek; Little Bourke Street for Chinese; Lygon Street, Carlton, for Italian; Victoria Street, Richmond, for Vietnamese; and Acland Street, St Kilda, for Jewish pastries. As well, the Colonial Tramcar Restaurant offers dining on its entire route!

Top: Hard Rock Cafe, Bourke Street. *Bottom:* Chinatown, Little Bourke Street.
Opposite: A menu designed to attract passers-by in Lygon Street, Carlton.
Pages 102-103: Borsari Restaurant in popular Lygon Street, Carlton.

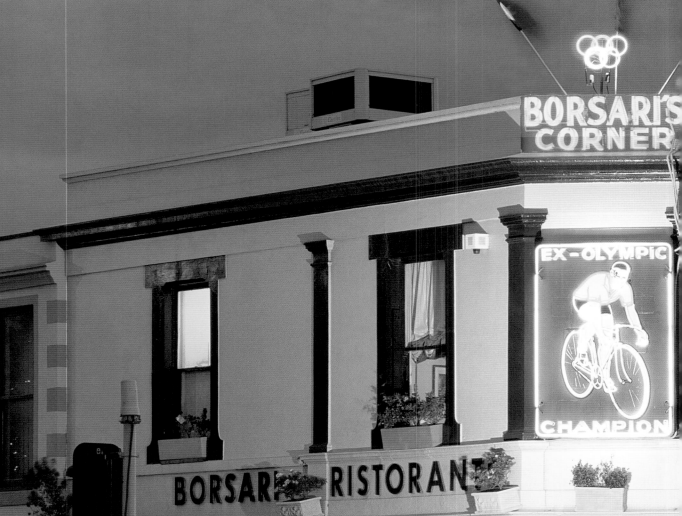

Above: La Camera Restaurant, Chapel Street, Prahran.

Above: Restaurants in Lygon Street, Carlton.

Melbourne's Suburbs

Like other Australian cities, Melbourne's suburbs sprawl away from the city centre well into the hinterland. This has put pressure on services and a policy of urban consolidation is being implemented in an attempt to accommodate an ever-expanding population. Here at Mentone, horticultural enterprises form a bulwark against encroaching development.

Above: An aerial view over Mentone showing the conflicting uses of land.
Opposite: Patterson Lakes, a popular canal estate.

Above: An aerial view of Carlton with the popular Lygon Street as it cultural heart.

Above: An aerial view of Fitzroy, a cosmopolitan haven for inner-city dwellers.

St Kilda

Fashionable again today, St Kilda has an interesting mix of architectural styles which reflect its chequered past. Acland Street has become a shopping and eating mecca, and on weekends Melbournians flock here to soak up the sun and take in the unique charm of the place. St Kilda has two distinct faces: Fitzroy Street is lined with take-away food shops and all-night bars, while Acland Street is a Jewish heartland, famous for its European cake shops and delicatessens.

Above: Looking north towards the city from the St Kilda Pier.
Opposite: An aerial view of the bayside suburb of St Kilda with Luna Park and the Palais Theatre in the foreground.

Top left: Acland Street, St Kilda's popular main street. *Top right:* St Kilda Pier promenade.
Bottom left: Bike Hire, St Kilda. *Bottom right:* Acland Street, St Kilda.
Opposite: Street stalls and the old Palais Theatre, St Kilda.
Pages 114-115: Sailing boats, St Kilda Pier and the city skyline.

Brighton

Further south from St Kilda is Brighton, a bayside suburb long popular for those seeking a holiday or day-trip destination. It is now also an affluent suburb offering city dwellers the luxury of living by the sea. The multi-coloured bathing boxes, which line the beach, allow their owners to leave possessions under lock-and-key for weekend sojourns.

Top: Sand follies, Brighton Beach.
Bottom: Soaking up the winter sun, Brighton Beach.
Opposite: Colourful bathing boxes line the beach at Brighton.

117

Above: An aerial view of Middle Brighton Pier, with sailing vessels.

Above: An aerial view of Brighton, the colourful bathing boxes lining the beach.

The Dandenongs

The Dandenong Ranges, just over 30 kilometres east of Melbourne, have for more than 100 years been a favoured day-trip destination for jaded city dwellers. Deep fern gullies and tall mountain ash forests provide a haven for wildlife, including the Superb Lyrebird, and contain cool glades in which visitors may picnic. On the south-eastern slopes, at the town of Belgrave, on the edge of Sherbrooke Forest Park, a narrow-gauge railway was re-opened as a tourist attraction in 1962. 'Puffing Billy' carries thousands of visitors annually on the trip between Belgrave and Emerald Lake. The little mountain towns of the Dandenongs are well-known for their gardens, plant nurseries, art galleries and antique shops.

Above: The Maroondah Highway near Healesville, winding its way through the mountain forests.
Opposite: Puffing Billy rounds the bend on its 13-kilometre journey from Belgrave to Emerald Lake.
Pages 122-123: Mountain Ash Forest, Yarra Ranges National Park.

Healesville Sanctuary

For over 50 years, Healesville Sanctuary has been committed to the care of Australian wildlife. Over the years, the Sanctuary has bred many species of Australian animals and today is involved in breeding programs for more than 20 species classified as threatened. Care is provided for orphaned or injured animals, many of which are returned to the wild. Visitors still flock to Healesville to get a good look at the Sanctuary inhabitants which include kangaroos, wallabies, koalas, platypuses, as well as a variety of bird species.

Above: A pair of Red Kangaroos at Healesville Sanctuary.
Opposite: Healesville Sanctuary is noted for its flourishing Koala colony.

Frankston

Frankston was once a popular holiday destination for Melbournians. In recent years it has grown to be a residential suburb connected to the city by a freeway, providing commuters with a seaside escape route. Nearby, Mt Eliza is an exclusive suburb at the head of the Mornington Peninsula, boasting good beaches and bracing sea air.

Above: An aerial view of Frankston.
Opposite: An aerial view of Mt Eliza and Pelican Point.

Mornington Peninsula

The Mornington Peninsula is Melbourne's seaside get-away, only a little over an hour's drive from the city. Its attractions include rugged surf beaches, tranquil, protected bayside beaches, rural hideaways, wineries, art galleries, tea houses, craft markets and stunning views. The seacoast is studded with opulent holiday homes and busy resort towns, and has a fertile hinterland. The Nepean Highway offers a direct route to the peninsula but the more scenic journey skirts the bayside suburbs of St Kilda, Brighton and Chelsea on the way to Frankston. From the small town of Dromana, past Mornington, a chairlift transports sightseers to the top of Arthurs Seat for fine vistas of the bay and ocean.

Top: A beach at Mornington Peninsula. *Bottom:* A pier off Mornington Peninsula.
Opposite: An aerial view of the Mornington Peninsula.
Pages 130-131: An aerial view of Cape Schanck, Mornington Peninsula.

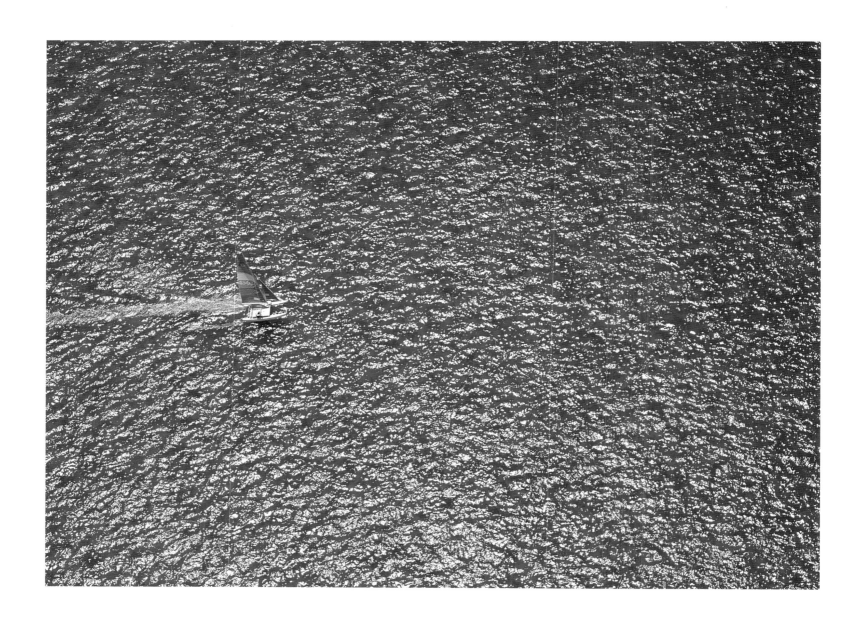

Above: A small sail cat skims the surface in Port Phillip Bay.

Above: At anchor in the waters of Port Phillip Bay.

Sorrento

Sorrento, not far from Point Nepean at the entrance to Port Phillip Bay, has long been a popular and fashionable beach resort. It was near here, in 1832, that an English lieutenant staked a land claim in the name of the reigning English monarch. Today, with neighbouring Portsea, Sorrento caters for weekenders and holidaymakers who feel far enough away from the city to unwind in this often wind-swept coastal idyll.

Above: Sunrise, Port Phillip Bay.
Opposite: Sunset, Back Beach, Sorrento.

Point Nepean

Point Nepean National Park was once home to a quarantine centre—now the School of Army Health. In the nearby cemetery, graves contain the remains of early settlers, shipwreck victims, military personnel and those who did not survive quarantine. Another remnant of the past, the old fort was built to protect the entrance to Port Phillip Bay. The walk from Point Nepean, via the Park to Cape Schanck, takes in the ocean beaches and unique coastal vegetation.

Above: Old fortifications at Point Nepean.
Opposite: An aerial view of Point Nepean.

Phillip Island

Phillip Island lies at the entrance to Westernport Bay and has been a popular resort since the 1870s. It is accessible by bridge, after a scenic drive down the Bass Highway, although some prefer the ferry trip from Stony Point to Cowes. The island offers spectacular scenery, excellent surfing and a wealth of wildlife. Favourites with visitors are the Little Penguins. During the breeding season they can be found incubating their eggs in burrows in the sand dunes. Australian fur seals also provide fascinating viewing for visitors to the island.

Above: Little Penguins coming to land at night to feed their chicks.
Opposite: A colony of Australian fur seals can be viewed from the Nobbies.
Pages 140-141: Cape Woolamai on the south-eastern tip of Phillip Island.

Williamstown

On the western side of Hobsons Bay, historic Williamstown, at the mouth of the Yarra River, was once the main sea port for Victoria. It has lately enjoyed a revival as a day-trip destination. On Sundays, ferries link Williamstown with St Kilda and the city centre. The most self-contained of Melbourne's villages, it is characterised by renovated iron-lace trimmed terraces and tree-lined streets and holds a popular weekend market specialising in local crafts. Visitors are treated to a variety of seaside cafes and seafood restaurants overlooking the water.

Above: A view from Williamstown across Port Phillip Bay to the city.
Opposite top: Williamstown Marina.
Opposite bottom: Nelson Place, Williamstown.

Bellarine Peninsula

Geelong, once the premier wool port of the nation, is today Victoria's largest provincial city, a commercial and industrial area and an important centre for education. The city has a large variety of fine old buildings including a monumental Town Hall. To the south and east of Geelong, the Bellarine Peninsula was important as a grain-growing region last century, although tourism and a small fishing industry are now the mainstays of the local economy. Historic Queenscliff, with its quaint guest houses and historic fort, is a popular holiday destination.

Top: Corio Bay, Geelong. *Bottom:* Point Lonsdale Lighthouse.
Opposite: An aerial view of Queenscliff, Bellarine Peninsula, looking north.

The Otway Ranges

The Otway Ranges stretch from the town of Anglesea to Cape Otway, dropping to Bass Strait in the south and extending to the volcanic plains of the Colac region in the north. Averaging 2000 millimetres of rain in their southern section, they support forests of messmate, manna gum and, at higher altitudes, the towering mountain ash and ancient myrtle beech. Otway National Park, proclaimed in 1981, extends over most of the Cape Otway peninsula and along the coastline to the west. Angahook-Lorne State Park, from Aireys Inlet to Kennett River, was declared in 1987 and includes areas of vegetation ranging from cool temperate rainforest to dry heathland. Picnic reserves and walks allow visitors access to enjoy the wildlife and verdant beauty of these forest areas.

Above: Temperate rainforest, Otway Ranges.
Opposite: Erskine Falls in Angahook-Lorne State Park.

The Twelve Apostles

From Princetown to Peterborough, the Great Ocean Road passes through Port Campbell National Park, renowned for its rugged coastal landscape. Limestone cliffs drop sheer to the Southern Ocean, constantly sculpted by waves into stacks such as the famed Twelve Apostles. London Bridge, Razorback Rock, Mutton Bird Island, the Bakers Oven and the Grotto are only a few of the fascinating geological formations along this 32-kilometre stretch of coast. The coastline is littered with shipwreck sites.

Above: Sunrise over the Twelve Apostles.
Opposite: An aerial view of the Twelve Apostles.

Sovereign Hill

The 1850s gold rush drew thousands of would-be miners from all over the world to the Victorian goldfields. Sovereign Hill was one of the richest mines—more than a quarter of the gold unearthed in Victoria came from Ballarat. At Sovereign Hill today, a recreated town functions as a 'living history' museum. Here visitors get a feel for a working gold town as people go about their daily chores dressed in period costume. The Red Hill Gully Diggings show how the first miners worked and lived before the town of Ballarat came into being. The reality of gold mining was that it was a tough, luckless existence for the majority, although a few struck it rich. However, the architecture of the towns of Ballarat and Bendigo is a reminder of the wealth that did flow from the mines and the buildings are examples from a golden era.

Above: Red Hill Photographic Rooms, Sovereign Hill.
Opposite: Street scenes from Sovereign Hill.

Bright

Once a centre for gold mining and later an important timber town, Bright has retained much of its past charm. Today, the annual Autumn Festival brings thousands of visitors to view the spectacular red and gold display of the broad avenues of elm, chestnuts, poplars and scarlet oaks. These deciduous trees were planted last century at the instigation of the Victorian Government Botanist. Set amidst the high country of the Victorian Alps, the town caters for hikers who attempt the many walks in the vicinity.

Above: Bright in Autumn.
Left: The town of Bright.

Winter in the Mountains

In winter, the Victorian Alps are a spectacular snow-covered landscape, the rugged terrain offering superb scenery. The Alps attract skiers to slopes which cater for downhill racing, cross-country skiing, snowboarding, tobogganing or simply enjoyment on skis. Mt Hotham, Mt Buffalo, Falls Creek, and other alpine localities offer resorts and amenities for all winter sports. In springtime and summer, visitors can bushwalk, fish the lakes and streams, ride horses or just relax in the mountain environment.

Top: Chairlift, Mt Hotham. *Bottom:* Skier, Mt Hotham.
Opposite: Victorian snow fields.

Country Victoria

Before gold was discovered and long after the boom had subsided, wool-growing was the industry that provided the economic backbone to the colony of Victoria. And it was the settled rural countryside that became the inspiration for the emerging Australian ethos of the 'bush'. Behind this mythology was the sweat of rural workers who toiled to fence the land, tend the stock and take the wool off the sheep's back. While life in rural Victoria goes along at a slower pace than in Melbourne, landowners today use modern technology in their agricultural pursuits to ensure a competitive edge in their production of commodities for volatile world markets.

Above: A shearer begins work on his next sheep.
Opposite: A country road, early morning.

157

The Murray River

The Murray River, which forms a natural boundary between Victoria and New South Wales, has long provided sustenance for Aboriginal people. For much of the nineteenth century, the river was a commercial waterway. By 1873, there were 240 vessels trading along the Murray and Echuca was a busy port. Eventually, however, railways took over the trade and only in recent times have paddle steamers returned as a means of transport for the delight of the many visitors who come to enjoy what the river and its towns have to offer. The river is also the source of water for the irrigated croplands of Australia's premier fruit-growing district.

Above: An aerial view of the Murray River near Mildura.
Opposite: An old paddle steamer on the Murray.

Acknowledgements

I n a book such as this it is possible to depict only some of the visual delights the city and environs have to offer. While I chose those images that seem to me to represent the essence of Melbourne, I could easily have filled a second book with pictures of marvellous Melbourne. I am indebted to Phillip Hayson for his assistance with the photography, Rod Ritchie for the text and Pip McConnel-Oats for the elegant design. Thanks also to Melbourne Zoo, Healesville Sanctuary and Sovereign Hill; to Crown Casino for extra photographs; and to the following photographers: Pauline Madden, page 6; Bill Bachman, pages 32-33; David Scaletti, page 81; Robin Smith, pages 80-81; Darren MacNamara, pages 94, 98-99; Diana Calder, pages 95, 138; Gary Lewis, pages 96-97; John Krutop, page 99; and David Callow, page 99.

STEVE PARISH CASEBOUND BOOK COLLECTION

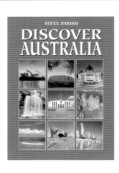
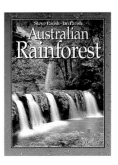
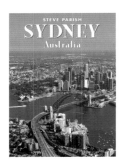

AVAILABLE AT ALL GOOD BOOKSTORES AND STEVE PARISH STOCKISTS

Steve Parish
PUBLISHING

© copyright photography and text Steve Parish Publishing Pty Ltd, 1996
Published in Australia by Steve Parish Publishing Pty Ltd
PO Box 2160 Fortitude Valley BC Queensland 4006 Australia

ISBN 1875932 25 9

PRINTED IN AUSTRALIA